T0350614

Notes on the Writing of
A Gentleman's Guide to Love and Murder

Robert L. Freedman

APPLAUSE
THEATRE & CINEMA BOOKS

Guilford, Connecticut

Applause Theatre & Cinema Books
An imprint of The Rowman & Littlefield Publishing Group, Inc.
4501 Forbes Blvd., Ste. 200
Lanham, MD 20706
www.rowman.com

Distributed by NATIONAL BOOK NETWORK

A Gentleman's Guide to Love and Murder
Book and Lyrics by Robert L. Freedman, Music and Lyrics by Steven Lutvak

Based on the novel *Israel Rank: The Autobiography of a Criminal* by Roy Horniman

All inquiries regarding stock and amateur rights should be addressed to Music Theatre International, 423 West 55th Street, New York, NY 10019. Robert L. Freedman c/o David Berlin, Schreck Rose Dapello Adams Berlin & Dunham LLP, 888 Seventh Avenue, 19th Floor, New York, NY 10106. Steven Lutvak, c/o Gil A. Karson Esq., Grubman Shire & Meiselas, P.C., 152 West 57th Street, 31st Floor, New York, NY 10019.

British Library Cataloguing in Publication Information available

Library of Congress Cataloging-in-Publication Data available

ISBN 978-1-4930-5598-2 (paperback)
ISBN 978-1-4930-5599-9 (e-book)

♾™ The paper used in this publication meets the minimum requirements of American National Standard for Information Sciences—Permanence of Paper for Printed Library Materials, ANSI/NISO Z39.48-1992

Printed in the United States of America

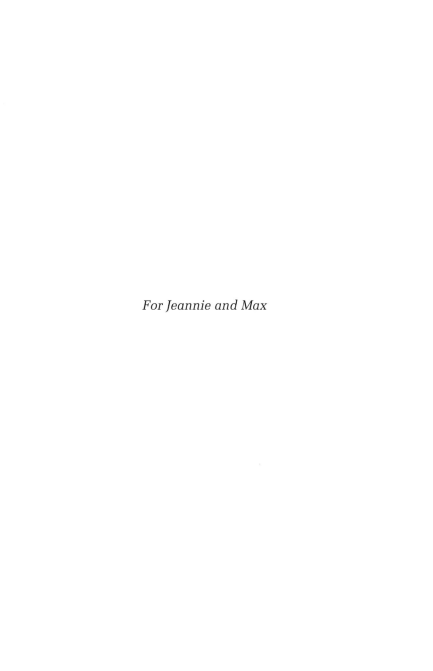

For Jeannie and Max

Contents

Prologue

In one moment, my life was now changed forever.
—Monty Navarro, Act I, Scene 5

1981: I met composer and lyricist Steven Lutvak when we were both students in the very first class of the new Graduate Musical Theatre Program at New York University's Tisch School of the Arts. Our faculty included Leonard Bernstein, Betty Comden and Adolph Green, Arthur Laurents, and Jule Styne. Guest speakers included Michael Bennett, Hal Prince, Stephen Schwartz, and Stephen Sondheim. There were sixteen of us, and we considered ourselves very lucky to be taught by these legendary masters of musical theater, especially at a time when there was great concern that the Golden Age of musicals was entirely a thing of the past, and that the genre itself was doomed to extinction.

Steve and I mostly worked with other collaborators at NYU, but we admired each other's work and talked about one day writing a musical together. About twenty years later, Steve approached me about adapting the 1949 Ealing Studios film *Kind Hearts and Coronets*, a droll comedy justifiably considered a classic in the UK, but relatively unknown in the United States except by ardent film buffs and Anglophiles. It is based on a witty and wicked Edwardian novel by Roy Horniman, *Israel Rank: The Autobiography of a Criminal*. Steve had seen the movie on TV and felt it was his destiny to turn this story into a musical.

It became my destiny, as well, when Steve, who would compose the music, asked me to write the book and cowrite the lyrics with him. With charm and persistence, Steve was able to persuade the rights holders to grant us, Broadway neophytes, the option to adapt the film, and we were off. The long journey to Broadway was a roller-coaster ride that took nearly ten years, and is enough to fill another book.

2013: *A Gentleman's Guide to Love and Murder* opened November 17 at Broadway's Walter Kerr Theatre. That night was the realization of a long-held dream. It changed my life forever.

What Does a Book Writer Do?

I trust you don't mind our being discreet.

—Asquith D'Ysquith Jr., Act I, Scene 6

The most frequently asked question about writing musicals is "Which comes first, the music or the lyrics?" As anyone knowledgeable about Broadway will tell you, the answer is: "The book." (Sometimes referred to as the "libretto," a familiar term in opera.)

And yet, as a young, aspiring book writer and lyricist, I received a very important piece of advice—a warning, actually—from Arthur Laurents, who wrote two of the greatest musical theater books of all time, *West Side Story* and *Gypsy*: "If you want to become famous, don't be a book writer for musicals."

He was right, of course. This is not so much a complaint as an observation. Theater lovers justifiably know the names of musical geniuses like Cole Porter, Rodgers and Hammerstein, Jerry Herman, Kander and Ebb, and

Stephen Sondheim, for example. It's never Bella and Samuel Spewack's *Kiss Me, Kate* or Howard Lindsay and Russell Crouse's *The Sound of Music* or Michael Stewart's *Hello, Dolly!*, Joe Masteroff's *Cabaret*, or Hugh Wheeler's *A Little Night Music*.

The Gershwins' Porgy and Bess was the actual title the last time *Porgy and Bess* was produced on Broadway, which apparently didn't leave room for DuBose Heyward's contribution.

With a couple of exceptions, Richard Rodgers and Oscar Hammerstein II's *Oklahoma!* (based on the play *Green Grow the Lilacs* by Lynn Riggs) is considered the first musical with an integrated book, with songs that spring from the story itself. Until then, most musicals were built around the songs and the stars, and their books were mostly a bunch of silly or clever gags and sketches, with maybe just enough of a plot to tie the whole thing together.

After the premiere of *Oklahoma!* in 1943, most musicals followed the Rodgers and Hammerstein formula of putting the story first, and crafting the songs, and creating the characters, to tell that story. There were often two love stories in these shows we now think of as traditional musical theater. The central love story involving the two leading characters, and a secondary love story involving another couple. It's a familiar trope. The story would be told in a linear fashion, with a beginning, which set up the plot and the main character's need or "want"; the middle, in which the character faces obstacles while trying to achieve their goal; and the ending, when the story is resolved, and the protagonist's goal is achieved (or, rarely, not).

This traditional kind of show went in a new direction in the late 1960s and early 1970s, with nonlinear storytelling and darker subject matter, as in three seminal musicals directed by Harold Prince: Kander and Ebb and Joe Masteroff's *Cabaret*, Stephen Sondheim and George Furth's *Company*, and Sondheim and James Goldman's *Follies*. Happy endings were no longer guaranteed. Other seminal shows like *A Chorus Line* (music by Marvin Hamlisch, lyrics by Ed Kleban, book by James Kirkwood Jr. and Nicholas Dante, directed and choreographed by Michael Bennett), and *Sweeney Todd: The Demon Barber of Fleet Street*, by Sondheim and Hugh Wheeler, also directed by Prince, followed.

By the time I started writing for the theater, I had seen, read, and absorbed these influential works, and many more classics that preceded and followed them. Not to mention countless biographies of the theater people I admired. I had two "bibles" when I was in college, which I wore out from repeated reading: *Act One* by Moss Hart, and *Sondheim & Co.* by Craig Zadan. Broadway was 3,000 miles away from where I grew up, in a tract house in a quiet suburb of Los Angeles, but it's where I wanted to be.

I did my first theater writing as a theater major at UCLA, writing one-act plays that were produced in the Little Theater on campus, and in my part-time job as a youth leader at a synagogue, where I wrote and directed musical parodies with a cast of teenagers. From there, I made a leap to graduate school at NYU. At that age, I still wasn't completely sure who I was or what I wanted to say, I just knew I wanted to say it with words and music. By the time I got my master's degree, it would be another twenty years before I had a show on Broadway. In the meantime, I wrote a couple of other musicals, but my day job was as a screenwriter in film and television, mostly dramatic movies and miniseries, but sometimes on musical projects (*Rodgers and Hammer-stein's Cinderella, Life with Judy Garland: Me and My Shadows*, both produced by the aforementioned Craig Zadan, and Neil Meron) while waiting for the opportunity to present itself to write for the musical theater. At a certain point, I realized no one was going to hand me the opportunity and I wasn't getting any younger. I was going to have to create the opportunity myself. And the only way to do that was to write a show. Enter Steven Lutvak and what would become *A Gentleman's Guide to Love and Murder.*

In this book, I attempt to give the reader a glimpse at creating a Broadway musical from a book writer's point of view. I don't presume to speak for anyone else involved (and yes, it takes a village, an entire community of artists in a variety of disciplines). This is simply my own, highly personal take on the process of writing and developing *A Gentleman's Guide.*

Story

And pigs might fly!

—Sibella Hallward, Act I, Scene 2

Figuring out what the story is might seem like a simple task when you're adapting a book or a film into a play or musical (or vice versa). You already know what it's about, right? Well, yes and no.

For me, the challenge is to find the elements I connect with. Sometimes it's the lead character. Sometimes it's the predicament a character is in. Sometimes it's an overriding theme that dovetails with my perspective on humanity, or society.

It's perhaps counterintuitive, but often you don't really know or understand what the show is about until you're actually writing it. As the story forms, and your characters start speaking, a theme (or multiple themes) may emerge. Sometimes, you don't realize what you've really written about until after you've finished a first draft. Sometimes, it happens when the show is in front of an audience. Sometimes, you don't realize what you've got until you hear someone else speak out about, or write about it.

Several things drew me to adapting the novel *Israel Rank* into what became known as *A Gentleman's Guide to Love and Murder*. For one, I found the dry wit and humor about a very dark subject appealing. In this story, especially, humor is used for irony, to critique the hypocrisy of society, and to mask or deflect deep feeling in a time and place where restraint and decorum were everything, and big emotions were kept hidden. As Monty writes in his memoir early in Act I, "It is a fact of life that no one ever tells the truth about himself." Ah, but in a musical, the truth can be revealed by putting a character's inner thoughts to music.

To my mind, this made the novel ideal for musicalizing. As a rule, you want characters in a musical to express themselves in song when mere dialogue isn't enough to capture what they're feeling. There are always exceptions to this, but it's what you need to consider when asking the question "Is this a musical?"

I loved the setting and period, Edwardian London. One thing that can work against you in a musical is the audience's lack of willingness to suspend disbelief. Does it make sense for a character to break into song, when that is not what most people do? (An exception may be made for musical theater geeks, many of whom, like myself, are in the habit of breaking into song at the drop of a hat.) For me, a bygone era or fanciful setting helps the audience with its suspension of disbelief. At times, contemporary costumes and sets can get in the way of losing yourself in a different world from the one you're living in.

There are many wonderful musicals set in contemporary times, of course, but there's usually a particular setting or point of view that sets it apart from everyday life. *The Book of Mormon* is one example. It takes place in the here and now, but at first you're immersed in the unique world of young male missionaries, and then in an African village that's just as foreign to the average audience. *A Chorus Line* is another example. When it opened on Broadway in 1975, it was immediate and contemporary. But you were thrust into the rarified world of Broadway dancers, a world with its own rules and traditions, as exotic in its own way as Siam (*The King and I*) or Anatevka (*Fiddler on the Roof*).

A very appealing aspect of the *Israel Rank* story was the novel's juxtaposition of a character who is always a perfect gentleman—but also a murderer. It's his gentlemanly behavior that keeps aristocratic society from suspecting him of foul play. In spite of everything he does, you somehow root for him. This is an aspect of the story that made it seem modern. What "old-fashioned musical" asks an audience to care about a serial killer? Of course, there are modern examples—*Sweeney Todd*, certainly. But while that masterpiece of musical theater is a gothic drama, albeit peppered with moments of humor along the way, *A Gentleman's Guide* would be a musical comedy.

If I had to pick one thing about the story I connected with the most, it's that it's all about an underdog. All his life, Monty Navarro has been dismissed and underestimated. No one believes he will amount to anything. And yet, by the end of the story, Monty has become the Ninth Earl of Highhurst, and he is treated with a deference and respect that was denied him from birth. I identified with that guy, and had a similar experience of feeling dismissed and underestimated growing up and as a young adult. What that created in me was the drive and the determination to make something of myself. I have since found this to be a rather common phenomenon, among creative people, and across the spectrum of experience.

Tied to that is the desire for revenge against those who have treated us ill. Most, if not all, of us can identify with that desire but, thankfully, very few of us act on it. In Monty Navarro's case, it's revenge against the eight relatives who have banished his mother to a life of penury and sorrow, and kept him from assuming his rightful place in society. From the beginning of time, we have told each other stories of evil people who have been vanquished.

So, as outlandish as this story is, and as far away from our time as Edwardian London may be, there is so much for a contemporary audience to identify with. It may be the reason *A Gentleman's Guide to Love and Murder* has resonated with so many people across the country and around the world.

Since so much of my writing experience involves telling other peoples' stories, real or fictional, and not my own, there was a time I wondered why I wasn't writing specifically about my own experience. After all, the first thing you're told in a beginning writing class is "Write what you know." In examining that, I came to realize that I have been writing about my own experience and emotional life from the very beginning of my career, without being conscience of it. All of my deepest feelings, my fears, my obsessions, my history, is woven into everything I write, and *A Gentleman's Guide* turned out to be no exception.

I have never murdered anyone, and what I know about Edwardian society I learned from books and movies. But I do know what it's like to be human. And I know about human interaction, and human frailty. And I know what it's like to be a son, a brother, a husband, a father, and a friend.

I had a sudden epiphany while we were in tech rehearsals at the Walter Kerr Theatre a few weeks before *A Gentleman's Guide* opened. I happened to be standing in an aisle watching our actors rehearse a scene in Act II set in the dining room of Highhurst Castle. The focus of the beginning of the scene is the bickering husband and wife, Lord Adalbert and Lady Eugenia. These are the first lines:

ADALBERT: This fish is an abomination!
EUGENIA: You specifically requested cod!
ADALBERT: She knows very well I detest cod.

It suddenly hit me, after years and years of working on the show, that I had written my parents. It actually came as quite a shock in the moment. But that dialogue exchange happened daily, in one form or another, when I was growing up in my parents' house, usually at the dinner table. My father would say to my mother, for instance, "How come you never make peas?" And my ever-patient mother would say, "You told me you hated peas, so I stopped making them." To which my father would gaslight us by saying, "I never said that. I love peas." And then the cycle would repeat itself, on and on.

Adalbert and Eugenia are (thankfully) a more extreme version of my parents. That scene had always been in the show and, until then, I never realized I was telling the story of my life within a musical about aristocrats in Edwardian England.

So, here you have a story about the British class system and the hypocrisy of Edwardian society. A story about an underdog who triumphs over adversity. A story about a young man who is denied the woman he loves. A story of a man torn between two lovers. A story about a woman who marries for wealth and position instead of for love. A story about a woman who marries a man she admires who is accused of murder. A story about a (mostly) dreadful, but wealthy and powerful family. A story about a criminal responsible for killing several relatives . . . who gets away with it. And all of these story threads are intertwined to form one larger story . . . about love and murder. That seemed like a challenging and delicious assignment. Would this story find an audience? We didn't know. We just knew that it was the story we were compelled to write.

Structure

Eight people would have to die for that to happen! How likely is that?

—Sibella Hallward, Act I, Scene 2

If there's one thing I want the reader to take away from this book, it's that a musical book writer doesn't just write dialogue, doesn't just write that stuff that comes between songs. I find it a common misconception about all dramatic writing, whether it's for theater, film, or television.

The chapter headings in this book give a sense of what the book writer contributes to a show. One of the most important, by far, is the story's structure. By this I mean the order of scenes, the revealing of plot and character, the relationship between scenes and songs. Each moment in a show is a building block to the next moment. It's cause and effect. If you think of, say, a snowball rolling down a hill that gets larger and larger, and goes faster and faster, until it makes impact, that's what has to happen with a show. Every moment has to push the story forward, develop characters, and build in intensity and momentum.

Some book writers go off and write a draft of the book, leaving spaces in the script for possible songs, and then present it to their collaborators. I prefer writing the book and score simultaneously, especially if I'm already writing or cowriting the lyrics. There is no right or wrong way, just what works best for you.

Whether for theater, film, or television, I usually start by writing down moments on 3 x 5 index cards. (Any size will do.) Each card might contain an idea for a scene, or for a character, for a line of dialogue, a song title, or any other element that comes to mind. At first, I write down ideas in the order they pop into my head, or that I glean from notes that I've taken, or from research. The ideas are random, at that moment, and don't tell me the order of scenes in the actual show. Not yet.

Once I've written a bunch of cards, I spread them out on a large table (or bulletin board) and, one at a time, I try to imagine the order these moments, scenes, and songs might take place. I place the cards in a kind of chronological order, even if, at some point, some scenes might come earlier and other scenes might end up being flashbacks. I might have a great idea for an opening, the end of Act I, or the finale. Those cards would naturally not be close to one another on the table.

When I've placed all the cards on the table, I see what's missing, where the holes are. And then, moment by moment, I fill in what has to happen to get from one plot point to the next. Gradually, and it may take days, or even weeks, I will fill the whole table with cards. Some cards will be moved, some combined into one scene, some discarded, and some put aside in case I find a spot for any of them later.

Brick by brick, to use another analogy, you build the show. It's only a blueprint at this point, a shape with which to look at the plot and see the whole picture at once. But it's still the very beginning. The next step is transforming the information on the cards into a document I can share with collaborator(s) and discuss.

I should point out that before I ever start writing out cards, I've already discussed the show and how I imagine it with my collaborator(s). In the case of *A Gentleman's Guide to Love and Murder*, that meant Steve and I agreeing, in general, on the kind of story we wanted to tell, the kinds of song we thought were right, the style and tone, tossing out ideas, getting excited and energized. Then, once we had our initial blueprint, the outline, we worked off that. The outline is never set in stone and, as we progressed, we changed things, we added things, we cut things, and the show gradually took shape as we worked. An outline is important because you've got to start somewhere. This is not the only way to work, it's just what works for me.

I believe you have to know how the story is going to end before you begin writing, even though that ending may change, or be very different from what you've first conceived. From the start, we knew there were going to be eight murders. We knew we wanted each victim to die a different, comical death. Ideally, the audience would look forward to each coming death, and we had to ratchet up the circumstances for maximum enjoyment. At the same time, we had to set up the premise and dramatize Monty's motivation. We had to weave the love story throughout. And the highlights of the story were all going to be musicalized. The songs had to be varied, ballads, up-tempo numbers, group numbers, solos. And not only would the songs have to move the plot forward, they also had to reveal character.

The show would be told in two acts, though telling it in one act without an intermission was certainly a choice we could have made, especially if we found there was no natural break between the acts.

In a two-act structure, where would we place the murders? Half in the first act, half in the second? Possibly. But as the show took shape, it became clear early on that once the murders started and happened regularly, the audience would be way ahead of us.

The first four deaths were large set pieces . . . the church tower (Reverend Lord Ezekial), the lake (Asquith Jr.), the bees (Henry), the trip around the world (Lady Hyacinth). By this time, the audience is on to us, so the next three murders are quickies . . . the accident in the gym (Major Lord Bartholomew), the backstage pistol (Lady Salome), and the heart attack (Lord Asquith Sr.). At the end of Act I, we have already killed off seven people (out of eight, total), and there's only one left, Lord Adalbert, the current Earl of Highhurst. We've also set in motion a love triangle between Monty, Sibella, and Phoebe.

During intermission, some may wonder what's left to happen in the second act if there's only one victim left. Because of the cards and the outline, we knew there was much more story to tell, once most of the murders were out of the way. The love story gets more complicated, and Lord Adalbert's murder leads to Monty's arrest and imprisonment. There are many surprises and reversals to come before the finale . . . and even after.

For me, an outline is necessary, an important guide, but it's malleable. It's meant to be changed when things aren't quite working. With each new scene and song, as the characters and scenes come to life, the show takes on a momentum of its own, and what you once thought was the perfect order may turn out not to be.

One thing that always amazes me, though it shouldn't, is that with each new project, there are always scenes I am absolutely certain are necessary and will always be there, and inevitably some of them get cut along the way. You have to be open and flexible and follow the show where it takes you.

Style and Tone

Sibella, has it never occurred to you to marry for love?

—Monty, Act I, Scene 2

How's that for understatement? One of the things that is most appealing about the novel upon which *A Gentleman's Guide to Love and Murder* is based is the droll, sophisticated voice of the narrator. The novel and the musical both use the device that our main character is writing his memoir from a prison cell on what may well be the eve of his execution. This makes the narrator's cool detachment all the more fascinating. It's not that the accused murderer doesn't wrestle with big emotions and deep thoughts—the man's life is at stake, after all—but that everything is presented with such startling understatement.

Monty first introduces himself in *A Gentleman's Guide* as the Earl of Highhurst. Everything about him, from his plush smoking jacket to his urbane reserve, tells us he is a wealthy aristocrat, to the manor born. But from there, the source material and the musical diverge.

As Steve and I began creating the show, we found that the character of Monty needed to be vulnerable as well as determined, enthusiastic as well as fearful, over-wrought as well as controlled. In short, Monty's mood and affect couldn't be ironic and detached. After we meet him in the prologue, he takes us back to his humble beginnings. Monty becomes a kind of every-man, searching for the things we all want in our lives, such as love, acceptance, and respect.

At the same time, Monty spends the greater part of the story assuming the attitude and demeanor of an Edwardian gentleman as he enters society and climbs his way up the ladder. His efforts to keep his emotions in check are an important part of the story, for his fate will be determined by his ability to create a persona that makes him utterly above suspicion even as murder victims pile up around him.

In evoking an Oscar Wilde kind of world, it was im-portant that we get the style and tone exactly right. In this we were eventually aided enormously by the brilliant design team chosen by Darko Tresnjak, who would become our director. When we started, however, what the show would look like was still very much in the air. Everything had to be evoked by the book, music, and lyrics alone. We had to create a world the audience would love as much as we did.

As we worked on the show, the humor expanded. We tried to make it as droll and witty and sophisticated as the source material. But as characters spoke, and sang, and interacted on the page, we were inspired to look for humor in everything. Not jokes or one-liners, per se, but humor that came naturally out of character and plot. One of the joys of creating the show was sitting in a room with Steve and laughing out loud as we tickled ourselves coming up with lyrics and wordplay, and veddy British expressions.

What started out as a show with reserved, sophisticated wit also became playful, silly, and laugh-out-loud funny, with more physical comedy than we imagined, initially. A lot of this had to do with the contributions of actors who brought our show to life, over time, with readings and presentations.

When Darko Tresnjak entered the picture, he brought with him his fertile imagination, talent for staging, and darkly delicious sense of humor ("I wasn't named Darko for nothing," says he), and heightened sense of theatricality.

Jefferson Mays, who got involved with the show four years before we got to Broadway, used his facility with voices and accents, his imagination and, indeed, his entire body to bring the many D'Ysquiths he played to life. Years before sets and costumes, he fearlessly threw himself on the floor when he fell from an invisible tower, crashed himself over music stands, raced back and forth across the room as he was pursued by invisible bees.

Darko leaned into the physical comedy, and by the time our first production opened at Hartford Stage in 2012, with the brilliant cast and direction, eye-popping production design, and Peggy Hickey's clever choreography, we had all the Edwardian style and sophistication we wanted and, a bit to our amazement, and our delight, we had become a full-out musical comedy.

Adaptation

I've developed a bit of a compulsion for beekeeping.

—Henry D'Ysquith, Act I, Scene 9

The first rule of thumb with any adaptation should be to ask yourself how you can make it your own, not how you can dutifully re-create the source material on which your adaptation is based. We've all seen theater, film, and television adaptations of books and stories we love and found them wanting. "It's not as good as the book" is a typical response, even when the adaptation is a success. Sometimes the problem is that the creators have attempted to copy the source material too closely, hoping to capture the magic of the original, trying to give the audience what they're expecting. Rarely does that approach work.

The way to make any material your own is to identify what in the story draws you to adapt it. Do you identify

with one of the main characters? Does the story dramatize something you have experienced? Does the story
reflect your own worldview? Does the story strike a
chord with you emotionally? Because musicals typi-
cally have such a long gestation period, which can be
all-consuming, you must ask yourself whether this is a
story you want to live with for years. Of course, this is
true whether it's an adaption or completely original.

While many projects are driven by commercial con-
siderations, especially adaptations of well-known,
tried-and-true titles, the chances of success are more
tied to the way the source material is adapted rather
than the built-in popularity of the title. The title may
get people into the theater, at first, but it's often no
guarantee of a successful run.

Israel Rank: The Autobiography of a Criminal is a
fairly obscure novel published in 1907 and written by
Roy Horniman, a popular writer of his day. Horniman
traveled in the same circles as Oscar Wilde, and their
style, as well as their desire to skewer the pretensions
of society, is quite similar.

When Steve and I began, the novel was in the public
domain. It had never been published in the United

States, and finding a copy was challenging. The long-deceased father of Israel Rank, the central character in the novel, is Jewish, which made his mother and he outcasts in Edwardian London. As with Israel and the "Gascoyne" family in the novel, in *A Gentleman's Guide to Love and Murder*, Monty's parents' marriage resulted in excommunication from the "D'Ysquith family." They were "cut off without a shilling."

Born to a life of "genteel poverty," Monty Navarro learns upon his mother's death that he is a member of the aristocratic D'Ysquith family, and thus a distant heir to a title and fortune. We follow Monty's journey to reclaim his birthright by murdering the eight heirs who precede him in the succession so that he may one day be Earl of Highhurst himself.

It should be noted that *Israel Rank: The Autobiography of a Criminal*, while a black comedy, is quite a bit darker in tone than *A Gentleman's Guide to Love and Murder*. Although the novel's Israel Rank is a very charming character, he is also quite devious and, more to the point, an unrepentant murderer with little or no conscience.

Subsequent appraisal after its publication has suggested the book is anti-Semitic. This may well be the reason that in the 1949 film adaptation, *Kind Hearts and Coronets*, Israel Rank's name is changed to "Louis Mazzini," and the character is half-Italian, rather than half-Jewish. It's been suggested in some commentary that making the character half-Jewish so shortly after the events of World War II would have been inappropriate and been met with justifiable criticism. In any event, we not only renamed the character for *A Gentleman's Guide*, but we changed his heritage to half-Castilian.

There are many characters in the novel that do not appear in *A Gentleman's Guide*, including Israel's mother, his father, Israel's friend and confidante Graham Hallward (Sibella's brother), and Lionel Holland, the man Sibella marries, who is spoken about in the musical but never seen. There are various other characters throughout that are not depicted in our adaptation.

Generally speaking, a novel allows you the breadth and time to have many more characters than you would choose to depict onstage. In a musical, it's necessary to focus on perhaps a handful of the characters, at most, which are crucial to the plot. Especially in this day and age, when musicals are so expensive to produce, you can't help but think about the size of your cast, and whether it makes producing your show prohibitive. (In our first production at Hartford Stage in Connecticut, we had a cast of eight, which was increased to ten when the production moved to the Old Globe in San Diego. For New York, we had a cast of eleven, still quite small by Broadway standards.)

At one time, early in our work, we met Monty's mother at the beginning of the show, and she had a lovely song, as well. As we worked on the show, it became clear that meeting her was delaying the beginning of the story, and we decided to get the story going after her funeral, instead. Even then, we discussed seeing his mother in a flashback or two. But each time we looked at the show as a whole, we realized that it would stop the plot in its tracks.

In the novel, the members of the D'Ysquith family in the line of succession before Israel Rank have (mostly) different names, and some have different personalities, and genders, than the characters in the musical. We often changed the names of characters large and small based on what sounded funniest to us. (Miss Shingle, another name that sounded funny to us, has no counterpart in the novel. She was created for *A Gentleman's*

Guide out of whole cloth, as were several other characters and situations.)

We also changed the names of places (Highhurst Castle instead of Hammerton, the winter resort at Chizzlemere instead of Lowhaven). I was constantly making lists of names and running them by Steve. I looked up popular names of the period, first names and surnames. Names in literature, and movies, names of real people and fictional. The renaming was actually very helpful in making these characters are own. It helped give us freedom to invent, not just character traits, but plot elements, as well. Gradually, during the time between when we began writing until we got to Broadway, the show got farther and farther from the source material, and became more and more our own invention.

Adalbert D'Ysquith, the current Earl of Highhurst, is a middle-aged man in *A Gentleman's Guide*. In the novel he is called Simeon Gascoyne, and is all of twenty-five years old when Israel Rank decides he will try to become Earl himself someday. He's recently married to an American heiress, and they are childless. Later in the novel, Israel discovers the troubling news that Lady Gascoyne has given birth to a son—another heir added to the line of succession.

To us, the names Asquith D'Ysquith and Asquith D'Ysquith Jr. are funnier than the characters' names in the novel—both are called Gascoyne Gascoyne. Otherwise, the younger men are similar: Gascoyne is twenty-seven years old, a young dandy prone to sow his wild oats. In *A Gentleman's Guide*, Asquith Jr.'s paramour is a certain Miss Evangeline Barley, a third-rate chorus girl. In the novel, she is called Kate Falconer, with a similar occupation.

Israel follows the couple to a hotel at a winter retreat where, after a false start or two, he poisons their tea and, while desperately worried he'll be noticed, ends up leaving no trace of ever having been there. In *A Gentleman's Guide*, Monty has "Poison in His Pocket," as his song is titled, but ends up causing the couple to (comically) drown in a lake.

Brother and sister Henry Gascoyne and Edith Gascoyne became Henry D'Ysquith and Phoebe D'Ysquith. In the novel, Henry dies in a horse-riding "accident" sinisterly devised by Israel. In *A Gentleman's Guide*, Henry now has a passion for beekeeping and is stung to death through Monty's clever manipulation. Having a swarm of bees onstage seemed both easier than having a horse and, we hoped, a great deal funnier. The bees and Henry's infatuation with Monty ("Better with a Man") are wholly invented for the musical. In the novel, Henry Gascoyne is a drinker who has gotten a village girl pregnant, and cruelly abandoned her.

The manners of death of each of the other D'Ysquiths were invented for the musical: The Reverend falling off the church tower, the Major decapitated by a barbell, for example. We made two of the D'Ysquith victims female: The society matron Lady Hyacinth, who perishes in a gangplank collapse (after escaping from cannibals); and the dreadful actress Lady Salome, who shoots herself with a loaded prop-gun backstage during her performance as Hedda Gabler.

In *Israel Rank*, by contrast, two of the victims are poisoned, one dies via arson, and one from deliberate exposure to diphtheria. Among other things, none of these methods of murder are particularly stage worthy or comical.

Every choice we made in our adaptation, every change, was dictated by what seemed the most theatrical to stage, and what tickled our funny bones. Remarkably, the further we strayed from our source material, the better the musical became. I believe this is because we made it our own.

For a deeper dive into the adaptation of the source material, *Israel Rank: The Autobiography of a Criminal* by Roy Horniman, has been republished and is easy to find.

Scenes and Songs

I am standing here with poison in my pocket.

—Monty Navarro, Act I, Scene 6

You have a plot. You have characters. Now, where do the songs go? How do you know what is dialogue and what is sung? As a general rule, it's ideal to have a character break into song when emotions are so high that mere dialogue isn't enough to express how they feel. But there are many other reasons to sing in a musical that are just as valid. If a musical takes place where music is already a part of the story, for instance, so much can be conveyed in a song. Even while it's presumably sung for an audience, there can be layers of meaning that reveal character and plot.

Musicalizing a story does not necessarily mean that dialogue and songs are separate, however. In most of the musicals I love, scenes and songs are woven together, musical numbers have dialogue interspersed throughout.

If you look at the score for *A Gentleman's Guide,* you will see very few songs that don't have dialogue woven through them. (For the recording, we eliminated most of the dialogue.)

The important thing is that, in a musical, the scenes and the songs are all telling the same story. Songs are not "plugged in" just anywhere, or interchangeable. They are germane to the plot. So much so that, if you were to read the dialogue without the songs, or listen to the songs without the dialogue, you wouldn't be able to understand the story.

That is why, in embarking on a collaboration with Steve, who most often writes both music and lyrics, I didn't want to just write the book. I wanted to write lyrics, too, because as a storyteller, I didn't want to have to write up to the most important moments, and then have to hand the story over to someone else. So, though Steve composed the music, and I wrote the book, we wrote the lyrics together, which I found very satisfying. By working in concert, it became easy and natural to weave the songs and scenes together.

The process went something like this: Once the story was outlined, we worked off that, even though we knew that, inevitably, things would change. But you have to start with a plan. The problem with writing a song before you have outlined the entire story is that, no matter how wonderful that song may be, you may find out later that the song doesn't fit into the story the way you may have imagined it would.

It's fine to start with the opening scene, but you may want to write it later, or even last, because it's the scene most likely to change once your show takes shape. There's a famous story about the opening number in the musical *A Funny Thing Happened on the Way to the Forum*, music and lyrics by Stephen Sondheim, book by Burt Shevelove and Larry Gelbart. The show was a comedy, but early audiences weren't laughing. Eventually they realized that the audience needed to be told it was a comedy at the very beginning. So, they cut their lovely opening number, "Love Is in the Air," and Sondheim wrote a whole new opening, "Comedy Tonight," which told the audience the kind of show they were about to see. From that point on, the show took off and the audience laughed the whole way through. And, literally, all that had changed was the opening.

We ended up writing several different openings for *A Gentleman's Guide*, some of them quite long and involved, with a lot of exposition, until we hit upon a very simple idea, kind of similar to what they did in *Forum*. We decided to prepare the audience for the show they were about to see ("Warning to the Audience"). It's brief, economical, establishes our tongue-in-cheek humor, and sets the audience up for the story that follows.

Shortly before our first Broadway preview, our producer, the savvy and indefatigable Joey Parnes, told us he wanted the show to open with more excitement. The opening had been working to our satisfaction at Hartford Stage and the Old Globe, but in the spirit of collaboration, we wrote something different (using some of the same music), and definitely more exciting. Almost immediately we realized what a mistake we'd made. Monty Navarro wakes up from a nightmare in which he's being hung and burned at the stake. We thought it was funny, but there was no way for the audience to understand that. It just looked like the beginning of a horror story, and so the audience was not set up to expect a comedy, and it affected the rest of the show. Clearly, it was the wrong solution to Joey's problem.

"You're a D'Ysquith" (Left to right: Jane Carr as Miss Shingle, Bryce Pinkham as Monty Navarro.) PHOTO BY JOAN MARCUS

"I Don't Understand the Poor" (Center: Jefferson Mays as Lord Adalbert; Ancestral Portraits, left to right: Jeff Kready, Jennifer Smith, Joanna Glushak, Price Waldman, Catherine Walker, Eddie Korbich.) PHOTO BY JOAN MARCUS

"Poison in My Pocket" (Left to right: Catherine Walker as Miss Barley, Bryce Pinkham as Monty, Jefferson Mays as Asquith D'Ysquith Jr.) PHOTO BY JOAN MARCUS

"Better with a Man" (Left to right: Jefferson Mays as Henry, Jennifer Smith as Pub Owner's Wife, Bryce Pinkham as Monty.) PHOTO BY JOAN MARCUS

"Why Are All the D'Ysquiths Dying?" (Mourners, left to right: Joanna Glushak, Price Waldman, Catherine Walker, Lisa O'Hare, Lauren Worsham, Jeff Kready, Jennifer Smith.) PHOTO BY JOAN MARCUS

"I've Decided to Marry You" (Left to right: Lisa O'Hare as Sibella, Bryce Pinkham as Monty, Lauren Worsham as Phoebe.) PHOTO BY JOAN MARCUS

"Barrel of a Gun" (Left to right: Eddie Korbich as Mr. Gorby, Catherine Walker as Servant, Lauren Worsham as Phoebe, Price Waldman as Servant, Jane Carr as Miss Shingle, Jefferson Mays as Lord Adalbert, Joanna Glushak as Lady Eugenia, Jeff Kready as Servant, Lisa O'Hare as Sibella, Jennifer Smith as Servant.) PHOTO BY JOAN MARCUS

"That Horrible Woman" (Left to right: Lisa O'Hare as Sibella, Eddie Korbich as Magistrate, Jeff Kready as Prison Guard, Price Waldman as Detective, Lauren Worsham as Phoebe.) PHOTO BY JOAN MARCUS

Once we put the original number back in, everything fell back into place.

As it happens, the first musical scene we wrote for *A Gentleman's Guide* was Sibella's introduction, "I Don't Know What I'd Do Without You." Sibella is telling Monty she doesn't know what she'd do without him, while her other words and actions are saying quite the opposite. In writing that song so early in the process, we were not only creating her character and moving the plot forward, we were setting the high style and sophisticated tone for the entire show. We had found the show's voice.

Early on, we wanted some of the score to reflect the musical styles of the era, such as music hall, Gilbert and Sullivan, and the like. (The orchestrations, by Jonathan Tunick, were completely acoustic, a rarity on Broadway these days, when nearly every show has amped-up electronic sound.) Similarly, we envisioned a production design that would feel like you were seeing a musical in Edwardian London, where the story is set, done (seemingly) without the high tech we're used to seeing in contemporary musicals. In the end, the production design was a canny mixture of high and low tech, which made the show feel modern and period at the same time. (Darko worked with a great team of designers to realize this vision, including brilliant production design by Alexander Dodge, evocative projections by Aaron Rhyne, spectacular costumes by Linda Cho, gorgeous lighting by Philip S. Rosenberg, expert sound by Dan Moses Schreier, fanciful period wigs by Charles G. LaPointe, and terrific makeup by Brian Strumwasser.)

Dialogue

Poison? In the port? Poppycock! I was in a position to know the Earl was dyspeptic and quite liverish.

—Miss Shingle, Act II, Scene 7

All of us speak dialogue every day of our lives. Therefore, it should be easy to replicate human speech. But if you really stop and listen to how people speak to one another, you'll hear right away that people rarely speak in perfect sentences. They often don't complete their thoughts, or jump to a new thought right in the middle of a sentence or even a word. Go to a coffee place one day, where everyone sits close to one another, and sit next to a couple that is engaged in conversation. Regardless of how mundane, it's a great exercise in hearing how people really talk.

The other important thing to notice about dialogue is that people rarely say exactly what they mean. In a typical scene in a play or movie, Character A wants something from Character B. It could be love, or the keys to the car. Maybe Character B isn't inclined to give it. The result is conflict, the basis for all drama. There are a hundred ways for Character A to try to get what they want without asking directly. Even when asked directly, Character B may say no. For instance, in the hypocritical society of *A Gentleman's Guide*, almost no one says exactly what they mean.

In a disagreement or fight with a loved one, they may be fighting over the car keys, but what they're really fighting about is their relationship, or control, or trust, or infidelity. All of this is first-year acting class stuff, to be sure. I think every writer should do at least a little acting to understand the process, and the approach to text.

A Gentleman's Guide to Love and Murder presented a different challenge altogether. This is culture where people often do speak in complete sentences. Many of the characters are erudite and sophisticated, not to mention clever and witty. This isn't a matter of listening to the way people talk in real life, it's trying to replicate the heightened style of Oscar Wilde or Noël Coward. In that regard, the novel was a wonderful source. Some lines of dialogue are taken directly from Israel Rank, as appropriate. More than specific lines, actually, the tone and style of speech in the novel helped us to capture the unique way people in Edwardian society spoke and interacted. And of course, other period novels, and films, were a constant inspiration.

We tried to have as much fun as possible with the dialogue and lyrics, leaning into period turns of phrase and idioms. The quote above from Miss Shingle at the trial is a good example. You'll notice the letter p is repeated for comic effect. I had the same kind of fun with character names like Pettibone, Pinckney, Pebworth, and Philpot. It was such a gift to have the latitude to capture a particular time and place through the language. I've had the same kind of satisfaction writing for 1934 and 1963 in other projects. But this was the most delicious.

Collaboration

Yes, I have looked death in the face. And death looked right back.

—Adalbert D'Ysquith, Act II, Scene 5

Theatre is a collaborative art form, and writers are indebted to the creative people who bring our words to life. When a book writer and/or lyricist works with a composer on a musical, it's almost like a marriage, with all of the issues and emotions that implies (but without the romance). You spend a lot of time in a room together and, because of the long gestation period of a musical, your lives and your futures are tied together.

For this reason, you want to find someone who is temperamentally a good fit with your personality. You want to work with someone you are on a more-or-less equal footing with, if possible, so you're not afraid of asserting yourself when the need arises. The process of writing and creating forces you to reach into your own heart and soul, at times, and to a certain extent, you have to be able to share yourself with your collaborator, and vice versa. If you're writing comedy, you want to find someone with a similar or, at least, compatible sense of humor.

Above all, you want to collaborate with someone with whom you are on the same page about the work you're creating. Do you see the show the same way? Do you agree on the style and tone? The musical sound? It's disappointing to see a show where the creators are at cross-purposes, where the book scenes don't mesh with the score, but it happens. It's not about talent, or just about talent. The collaborators each have to be writing the same show.

Steve Lutvak was a good collaborator for me for a number of reasons. We enjoyed each other's company, and had a similar sense of humor. Two more things turned out to be essential. First, we both saw the show the same way. And second, Steve is smart, and a natural storyteller himself. He's someone I could talk about the story with, and bounce off ideas. And he could do the same with me. We're not alike in so many other ways, but our differences somehow complemented each other.

On the bumpy road to Broadway, we always had the same understanding of what we were writing, and what we wanted the show to be.

And we had fun. When writing lyrics together, trying to come up with rhymes or Britishisms in our faux-British accents, we spent hours on end cracking each other up. Lyric writing is a little like puzzle-solving, and it was good to have a partner to figure out all the intricacies of the craft.

For the first several years of our journey with *A Gentleman's Guide*, we were on our own. No producer, no director (except for a workshop at the Sundance Theatre Lab led by the wonderful Ron Lagomarsino), no one but ourselves to believe in the show enough to stick with it. We did have some encouragement along the way. The Huntington Theatre in Boston provided us with our first full reading of the show, in 2006. That same spring, we won the Kleban Award for lyric writing, which came with a monetary prize. That summer, we got tremendous support from the Sundance Theatre Lab. And that fall, we won the Fred Ebb Award for songwriting, which also had a cash prize. Steve was a Jonathan Larson Fellow, as well. Even with all of that support and encouragement, we weren't able to secure a producer or a production of the show.

After about five years, we had a lucky break. The director Darko Tresnjak read the script, listened to the score, and found it to be right up his alley. We met, we talked, we decided we'd make a good team. We were confident we were all seeing the same show. At the same time, Darko brought a new set of eyes and ears to the project which was very welcome. He was brimming with ideas. At the time we met, Darko was the co-artistic director of the Old Globe theater in San Diego. Within a year or so, he became the artistic director of Hartford Stage in Connecticut, and wanted to direct *A Gentleman's Guide* in his first full season, as a coproduction with the Old Globe.

Now we had two regional theaters and a director we loved. By this time, Darko had already suggested Jefferson Mays to star as the D'Ysquiths, so we also had a magnificent Tony-winning actor to star. There's a saying that luck happens when preparation and opportunity come together. After so many years developing our show, we were prepared. When the opportunity presented itself, we were ready for some luck.

With a production looming, Hartford Stage gave us a workshop to get the first act up on its feet so we could see what we had. We had a terrific and game cast; Darko, our fearless leader; and his longtime choreographer, Peggy Hickey. A couple of memorable things happened that snowy winter week which help illustrate what collaboration is all about.

There's a scene in the show where Monty has followed young Asquith Jr. and his paramour to a resort. In the song, "Poison in My Pocket," Monty contemplates how he might execute his mission. As he grows more anxious by the minute, he contemplates poison, but doesn't have the opportunity. We wrote many versions as the method of murder kept changing. At one point in the writing of the song, Monty disabled the brakes on a motorcar sending the unsuspecting couple off a cliff to their doom. By the time we got to the workshop at Hartford, we had Monty taking over a Ferris wheel at a county fair. He accelerates the speed so much that the two victims are sent flying to their death from high atop the ride.

We were rehearsing with the actors at the piano in a large rehearsal room, and Darko was listening. As the song progressed, Darko started moving across the room as if he were ice-skating. The rhythm of the song seemed perfect for that action. Long story short, we were now on a frozen lake, the lyrics changed once again, and the doomed couple perished falling into a hole in the ice (sawed by Monty) while skating. It became one of the most memorable moments in the show.

Over a year later, we were in a rehearsal studio in Manhattan, preparing for Broadway. Darko came over to me with a mischievous glint in his eye and said, "What if Lady Salome's severed head rolls onstage from the wings after she shoots herself." I should digress by saying that I was of the mind that the show should never get gruesome, and that we should keep the murders funny, not horrifying. So, my first reaction was no. And then, after giving it more thought, I realized that after you shoot yourself in the temple, your head might explode, but it wouldn't be decapitated. Darko agreed, and then came up with a wacky but brilliant idea to have the now-bloody feathers of Lady Salome's costume be shot out of cannon from offstage, covering the other actors with feathers as they take their bows at the end of *Hedda Gabler*.

But Darko wasn't finished with decapitation. In a scene where Major Lord Bartholomew drops a bar of weights on his neck and breaks it, Darko suggested his head roll out onstage. Again, my gut was reaction was no, but Darko persisted and said he'd get the crew to rig it up, and then I'd be able to see whether I liked it or not. The next time I watched the scene being rehearsed, Darko was ready. I sat there thinking, "Well, to be a good collaborator, I'll let Darko give it a shot. But it's too gruesome."

Then the barbell falls, and suddenly the bloody decapitated head pops out onstage from behind, and it was the funniest thing I had ever seen in my life. It was startling, and I absolutely loved it. It stayed in the show. Maybe it was too silly to be truly grotesque, all I know is it tickled me no end, and continued to do so during the entire run. Thank heaven for Darko's persistence. We trusted each other enough to give each other the space to experiment and try new things.

Casting

When I think of the indignities you've suffered.
—Phoebe D'Ysquith, Act I, Scene 10

The director Elia Kazan and others have been quoted as saying that 80 percent of directing is casting. A writer has a blank page in front of him, with characters to create, a long time before there is any thought of casting. Occasionally, if you are in a position to write for a particular actor or star, you have the luxury of hearing that person's voice in your head, and you have the opportunity to write to that actor's unique strengths. When I was writing the ABC miniseries *Life with Judy Garland: Me and My Shadows* (2001), adapted from a book by her daughter, Lorna Luft, I had the advantage of the film and television performances of the great Judy Garland herself to think about while "creating" the character. I also had quotations in the book, and in interviews Garland gave over the years. I even had a top secret (at the time) tape recording of Judy Garland speaking about herself at a particularly troubling time near the end of her life. But my secret weapon was knowing that the producers intended to cast the actress Judy Davis as Garland. I'd been a fan of hers for a long time, and I ended up taking inspiration for the grown-up Judy in the script from both the real Judy Garland and Judy Davis the actress. It was no surprise that Davis, as well as Tammy Blanchard as Young Judy, both received Emmy Awards for their performances. In the many television films I've written, Judy Davis is the only actor to ever deliver my dialogue exactly as written, including every pause and ellipsis (. . .) in the script, a rarity for film and television, in my experience.

Actors are a great gift to writers. Hearing your words spoken out loud, even in a cold reading, can reveal multitudes. The same goes for hearing your songs performed. Actors give you insight into ways characters and dialogue can be interpreted differently than what you may have heard in your head while writing. Your characters, your whole story, can grow exponentially through the participation of a gifted actor who can show you the way. I can't explain it, but some actors just seem to "get" what you're going for instantly. Of course, actors work on material in different ways. Some actors show up to the first day of rehearsal with a specific interpretation of the character all worked out ahead of time. If such a prepared actor interprets a line of dialogue differently than the creative team imagines, sometimes it's actually better their way. If not, an adjustment from the director (or a rewrite from the author) sets everything right. Other actors arrive without thinking things through ahead of time and let the script, the director, other actors, and the rehearsal process help them find the character eventually. Ideally, we are all embarking on this journey together and "discovering" the show together as it reveals itself to us. No matter how skilled and seasoned a writer may be, there are always changes when the actors and the director and choreographer get the show up on its feet. Once a writer shares the script with the creative team and the actors, inspiration can lift the material to a higher level. There's nothing more exciting than seeing your work become better than you imagined in collaboration with great artists.

I adore actors. They put themselves on the line, naked and vulnerable, in front of producers and directors and writers and casting directors who are there to judge them. It's not an easy life, and handling rejection is a big part of it. I admire actors so much for their talent and perseverance, and also for the love and support they give to each other. Most of the actors I know are warm, big-hearted, and very, very hard working.

What I hope all actors realize is that when they come to audition, everyone sitting at the table hopes they will succeed, hopes they will be perfect for a role. Sometimes actors change your mind about how you perceive a role just by the audition they give. Actors trudge to auditions, in freezing temperatures, and in unbearable humidity, and after long (and costly) days and hours of preparation, and are expected to be breezy and delightful and convince you they are someone you'd love to work with—no matter if they've had a bad day, if their cat has died, if they've been evicted, you name it. Once inside the audition room, no one wants to know your personal struggle to make it to this moment. Actors have the toughest job in show business, by far.

A Gentleman's Guide to Love and Murder posed some great casting challenges. Every single one of the cast of eleven had to be able to embody the very specific

Edwardian style of all the characters, including British accents and royal bearing. And they had to have wonderful voices in a variety of ranges, and be fabulous actors, as many of them had to play multiple roles.

First and foremost, one actor was required to play eight (well, actually nine) members of the D'Ysquith family. The actor had to be larger than life, with some indefinable star quality. He had to be funny. He had to be physically adroit. He had to have classical training. He had to embody a rogues' gallery of loathsome characters, people you love to hate. And, of course, he had to know how to put over a song with the best of them.

In the years when we were writing and developing the show, Steve Lutvak and I tossed out names of actors we admired and thought would be right for the D'Ysquiths. Many of them were Brits, naturally. Shortly after Darko Tresnjak came on board to direct the show, he said he had someone in mind, an actor he had worked with at the Williamstown Theatre Festival a few years earlier: Jefferson Mays. Both Steve and I were gobsmacked. Of course! Jefferson Mays would be perfect! A Best Actor Tony winner (for Doug Wright's *I Am My Own Wife*), he had all the qualities we needed, both on stage and, as it turned out, off stage, as well. He's as kind, generous, and thoughtful a human being as you'd ever want to meet. I daresay, you will never meet another actor as dedicated and hard-working. What's more, Jefferson is quite an Anglophile, as well as a great student of history, literature, and art. He turned out to be an inspiration to me in many ways, not least of all with his vast knowledge of the era, language, and world of *A Gentleman's Guide*. I think of him as more than an actor or a star, but also as a collaborator, because he was that, and more. From the very first reading of the show with Jefferson in the lead, he invested each character with his or her own voice, physicality, and personality, scrupulously following the script and yet making each one of the D'Ysquiths come alive in often surprising and hilarious ways. Even off stage, Jefferson seems like a gentleman from another, lovelier and more elegant, era, and he brought all that and more with him on stage. For readings, he even pulled a variety of appropriate hats out of his own impressive collection to help delineate each character.

Some have pointed out that the D'Ysquiths is the starring role, but that the role of Monty Navarro is the actual leading role in *A Gentleman's Guide*, and that is true. Monty is the protagonist of the story, and it his journey that we follow. Monty, as has been noted, is also a serial killer. The question was, from the beginning of the writing process, how do we make Monty likable enough for the audience to root for his success? Otherwise, no one would care about him, and we wouldn't have a show. In the creation of the role, we did everything we could to make Monty sympathetic (and to make all the D'Ysquiths loathsome). But we knew we would have to find an actor for the role of Monty who the audience would fall in love with. Sure, he'd have to be handsome and charming, but also vulnerable in the early scenes, and masterful by the end. And, of course, he'd have to be a wonderful singer, a gifted actor, and embody the high-style of the show. For Broadway, we cast Bryce Pinkham, and he served up great charm, comic agility, a gorgeous voice, and all the heart and pathos required, and more. Audiences embraced him, and he was nominated for a Tony. One of his fellow nominees, of course, was Jefferson Mays. (For the record, the award that year went to Neil Patrick Harris in *Hedwig and the Angry Inch*.)

The two leading female roles, Sibella and Phoebe, both had to be played by sopranos, rather rare for a Broadway show in an era of big belters. We cast two women who are both megatalented, and knocked the audience's socks off every single night. Sibella was played by the marvelous Lisa O'Hare, a British actress who perfectly captured Sibella's allure, her intelligence, her wiles, and made you fall in love with a selfish, self-involved character. Phoebe was played by the fabulous Lauren Worsham, funny and winsome, with some tricks up her sleeve, as well. Lisa and Lauren both have gorgeous voices, and together and alone, made their songs soar. Just as important, they are both very fine actors, and did more than justice to Linda Cho's gorgeous (and Tony-winning) Edwardian-meets-steampunk costumes.

The character of Miss Shingle is a small but pivotal role. She starts the show, and we needed a unique actress with great charisma to pull off all the exposition required of her number, "You're a D'Ysquith." I had always imagined someone like Jane Carr, a British actress I'd long admired, from her first film *The Prime of Miss Jean Brodie*, to the Royal Shakespeare Company, *Nicholas Nickleby*, and beyond. I couldn't believe our luck when we didn't just get a Jane Carr type, but the actual Jane Carr herself, in the flesh. And she was absolute perfection.

Playing multiple roles, we were fortunate to have an ensemble of actors, each of whom could, and do, play leading parts all the time. Each and every one of them is unique, and each of them raised the level of the show just by being in it. Every one of these marvelous actors had at least one stand-alone moment to shine, and even made their smaller roles memorable: Eddie Korbich, Jeff Kready, Joanna Glushak, Jennifer Smith, Price Waldman, and Catherine Walker. During the run, we were fortunate to be joined by Judy Blazer, Jennifer Blood, Pamela Bob, Jordan Bondurant, Sandra DeNise, Kristen Hahn, Greg Jackson, Amy Justman, Mark Ledbetter, Barbara Marineau, Kevin Massey, Michael McCorry Rose, Carole Shelley, Jim Stanek, Don Stephenson, Scarlet Strallen, and Kathy Voytko.

It would be impossible to name all the wonderful performers who did the national tours of *A Gentleman's Guide*. I do feel I must include all of the unsung heroes of the show's development over nearly ten years before opening on Broadway. Dozens of dedicated actors helped us create their characters in various readings, workshops, and out-of town productions, too many to mention; but a special debt of gratitude is owed to the brilliant Nancy Anderson, Ken Barnett, Robert Petkoff, Chilina Kennedy, and Tregoney Shepherd.

Epilogue

Glorious days, glorious days.

—Reverend Lord Ezekiel D'Ysquith,
Act I, Scene 4

Everything that happened with *A Gentleman's Guide to Love and Murder* during the 2013–2014 Broadway season was both wonderful and surreal. Our reviews were better than we ever could have imagined in our wildest dreams. As awards season got under way, we received eleven Outer Critics Circle nominations (we won four, including Best Actor, Best Director, and Best Book), twelve Drama Desk nominations (we won seven, including Best Book and Best Lyrics), the Drama League Award, and ten Tony nominations (we won four, including Best Director, Best Book, and Best Costume Design). We won Best Musical from all of them.

In the fall of 2015, a National Tour went on the road for eighteen months. After that closed, a non-Equity National Tour went out for another nine months. Two years and two months after opening, we closed on Broadway on January 17, 2016, having had 905 performances and thirty previews. In May 2018, *A Gentleman's Guide* was licensed for regional theaters, community theaters, schools, and colleges. In 2019 alone, there were about seventy-five productions across the United States and Canada.

So far, there have been productions in Australia, Japan, China, South Korea, and Sweden. A production in the UK is in the planning stages.

Sometimes when the show was running in New York, if I was in the neighborhood, I'd pop in and watch the last ten or fifteen minutes. There's nothing in the world like the feeling when people react to the show at the end. The overwhelming excitement of the audience, the incredible enthusiasm, it's thrilling. It's *the* thing about the show that's the most meaningful to me; feeling that from the audience and knowing that I've been a part of it, of a shared experience like that. There's nothing like it in the world. And, as exciting as winning my Tony was—and I don't mean to in any way diminish that, it was amazing and somehow, unreal—but that feeling from the audience was miraculous and wonderful and moving to me every single time.

At the beginning, when we started writing the show, nobody else cared whether we wrote it or it ever got produced. It was our belief in the show and in ourselves that kept us going all those years. To me, the show's success is proof that dreams do come true.